Gustaf Munch-Petersen

Selected Poems

Gustaf Munch-Petersen

Selected Poems

Bilingual Edition
Translation © 2009 by Brian Young
New Nordic Press

First edition 2011
ISBN 978-0-615-55275-0
Library of Congress Control Number: 2011941414
Published by New Nordic Press
Port Townsend, WA 98368

N N P

Printed by Lightning Source
La Vergne, TN 37086
Printed in the Unites States of America

Ursula Munch-Petersen—A Daughter's Tribute

Gustaf Munch-Petersen is my father. He was only 26 years old when he died, and it seems strange that he is still being published and read, not just in Danish schools, but now also in America.

Besides his poetry, he left behind two daughters– my sister who was two at the time, and me, not yet born. My sister Mette got married in Norway and had five children, and eight grandchildren. And I have two sons and three grandchildren.

It says in the Bible that the sins of the father are passed down through seven generations. All of Gustaf's grandchildren have been marked by their grandfather's absence, while at the same time he is proclaimed a hero. My sister felt betrayed, and has spoken very little about her Danish childhood. And now her children are asking me about it.

I have often thought, when I felt sad, that there was something waiting in Heaven–some kind of inheritance. When, as an adult, I read for the first time the book *Primitive Religion* by the Danish religious historian and linguist Vilhelm Grønbech, I experienced clearly my relationship to my father. My grandma had told me that Gustaf was tired of school, and that he would only take lessons from Vilhelm Grønbech, who wrote extensively about so-called "primitive religions." My father's insistence on taking lessons from Vilhelm Grønbech, and my joy and surprise when reading about the world's religions as an artistic aspect of my life, helped me to feel a connection to him.

Every time a soldier is killed in Afghanistan I think about the far reaching consequences for the families. But that my father's poetry is still being printed and read, and because he felt it was an extension of the concept of art, and that he took his feelings and thoughts so seriously that he went to Spain when war was on the rise, that gives his fate meaning.

In 1937 you could still believe in the promise of the international participation for the defense of the Spanish people. Last year I was in Spain where now– and first now– one can talk openly about the civil war. A museum there had a collection of photos of all of the international brigades. There were volunteers from India and China, which surprised me, that people from so many places in the world came to fight.

I don't know what young soldiers today are thinking when they say that they are going to war to "Make a difference", but death in modern warfare must be even sadder and more meaningless today than it was then.

Ursula Munch-Petersen, October 2011

Introduction

Gustaf Munch-Petersen was one of Danish literature's "young dead". He died at the age of 26 as a volunteer in the Spanish Civil War, fighting on the side of the Republicans. The tragic story of the young poet, who fights and dies for his ideals, appeals directly to both the emotions and the imagination. For that reason, in the first decades after his death, he became at least as well known for his dramatic fate as for what he had written. During his life he had been unable to make his mark as an author. The Selected Poems, which was published after his death in 1938, was the first of his books to get a unanimously positive reception. But in general, critics concentrated more on his participation and death in the Spanish Civil War than on his poetry. However, he eventually became accepted in the literary milieu, and in the period following the Second World War he came to be considered a leading figure in the lyrical modernist movement in Denmark. With his openness to the international aesthetic movements, and his untraditional use of language, he had, in fact, been out in front of most of his contemporary Danish colleagues.

Gustaf Munch-Petersen, who was born in 1912, grew up in a well-to-do family in the Copenhagen academic class, together with two younger brothers. His father was a professor in engineering science and his mother, who was from Stockholm, was a professor in Swedish literature at the University. His parents had big expectations for their oldest son, who had both creative and academic abilities. It was expected that he would continue his studies after high school. He started to study psychology, and then art history, but those studies could not hold his interest for more than a few months at a time. He painted and drew since childhood, and started to write poems while still in high school. Art and poetry became early on the things that he recognized as his real work, even though he was never able to earn a living working at them. For some months he earned money working as a miner in Greenland, but for the most part he relied on financial support from his parents, and that made it possible for him to concentrate on his writing, and to get inspiration from trips to Sweden and Italy. He lived on the island of Bornholm from 1935, and the island's nature played an important role in several of his later poems. It was on the island of Bornholm that he married the potter Lisbet Hjorth, with whom he had two daughters.

Even though Gustaf Munch-Petersen's work was completed within the span of a few short years, it is surprisingly varied. He experimented with several different movements, such as vitalism, surrealism, and primitivism. Also such diverse influences as social realism and Christian mysticism had an influence on his work. But his experimental way of writing was not appreciated in the Danish cultural life of the 1930's, which was aesthetically conservative. Simply the fact that he wrote in unrhymed verse, and as a rule used only lower case letters, was seen as provocative by many of the established critics of the time. From the very beginning he saw himself as an artist who belonged to the avant-garde, the vanguard that should fight against the inhibitions of tradition, and find a new way forward, towards something new and emancipating. Although he was sometimes plagued by doubt, most of the time he was convinced that art could change the world. Many of his poems describe utopian visions of a very different future, one that could be made possible by both outer, and especially inner, changes in mankind. The longing for a radically different reality can be seen in much of what he wrote, and that feeling was a driving artistic force within him. His sympathies were politically on the left, but he was interested mostly in ideas and art, and he was not actively engaged in any organized political movement. For that reason it came as a surprise to his family and friends when he decided to fight in the Spanish Civil War. But in the letters that he sent home from Spain, he writes that he saw his participation in the war as a continuation of his artistic work. In that sense the avant-garde struggle for what he hoped would bring about a better world, had to take place with real weapons in the end, and no longer with pictures and words.

Martine Cardel Gertsen
Copenhagen, March 2010

Tom Kristensen- Et Mindedigt

Nogle Linjer
til min Ven Gustaf Munch-Petersen
som faldt i Spanien

Pludselig ser vi det hele.
God er en pludselig Død.
Pludselig ser vi, hvad halsløs,
tankeløs Ungdom betød.
Kort var din hastige Vej fra
Kroppen og Tanken til Ord.
Kortere endnu din vej
fra Liv til den støvede Jord.

Ordene kom fra det Indre,
ingen af os kan forstaa.
Ingen Besindigheds Vægte
bærer dit Prosadigt paa.
Det, som du sagde, var Sandhed
samme Sekund, det blev til;
ikke et tænksomt: jeg tænker;
kun et halsløst: jeg vil.

Her skal vi andre nu vandre
gennem et Ælte af Kunst,
blive en kedelig Gældspost
uden Mæcenernes Gunst,
blive en Støvhob af Gloser
skrevet af Tvang og af Pligt,
medens du hviler, skudt ned, skudt ned,
dit Livs ubesindigste Digt.

Tom Kristensen – A Tribute

A few lines
To
My friend Gustaf Munch-Petersen
Who fell in Spain

Suddenly we see it all,
A sudden death is good.
Suddenly we see, what reckless,
Thoughtless youth could.
Short and quick your path
From body and thought to poem
And shorter yet your path
From life to dusty loam.

The words came from deep inside,
None can know that source.
No sober minded lofty thoughts
Your poems need put forth.
What you told, became the truth
As soon as it was said,
Not a thoughtful: let me think,
Just a reckless: I intend.

Here we others wander still
Through a mire of Art
To just run up a boring debt
Without Maecenas's heart,
To become a dusty pile of words,
By force and need atoned,
While you rest, shot dead, shot dead,
Your life's most reckless poem.

Translator's note:

Thirty-four of the poems in this volume are found in *Udvalgte Digte* (Selected Poems), first published in 1938 by Fischers Forlag, and again in 1962 by Gyldendal. Those were taken from four previously published works: *Det nøgne Menneske* (The Naked Man)1932, *Det underste land* (The Lowermost Land)1933, *Mod Jerusalem* (Towards Jerusalem)1934, and *Nitten Digte* (Nineteen Poems)1937.

Besides the 34 Danish poems, translated here, there are eight English poems in *Udvalgte Digte*. They were included in the unpublished collection *Black Gods Stone*, written in English.

I translated these poems line by line, retaining, as far as possible, the original format and punctuation. Gustaf Munch-Petersen wrote with a unique style, making up some of his own words, and using common Danish words in an unusual manner. Some of his contemporaries said that he was hard to understand. The poems have their own characteristic form of expression in both Danish and English.

Gustaf Munch-Petersen was born on February 18, 1912, and died in March of 1938 as a volunteer in the Spanish Civil War. He was just 26 years old.

I want to thank Martine Cardel Gertsen for her support, and Ursula Munch-Petersen for providing a tribute to her father. Ursula was not yet born when Gustaf left to join the International Brigade in the fight against Fascism in Spain. Gustaf left Denmark on November 8, 1937, and Ursula was born on December 29. Gustaf received the news about his new daughter at the end of January, 1938. They never saw each other.

Brian Young
Port Townsend, WA
November, 2011

March 26, 1938
At the front in Aragon, Spain
Gustaf Munch-Petersen's last letter home to
Lisbet.

The entire world is one front— for or against the beautiful life, that man could live. Each and everyone, wherever they might be, must understand that, in spite of the struggle, it is so precious and great, that it shall be saved, no matter what it costs— that nothing can have any meaning, if that is lost on Earth. We must face the reality, that the most simple thing, that our life requires, demands the greatest struggle, and the greatest sacrifice from us....

List of Poems

The Selected Poems

Søvne

jeg elsker dig ikke
men jeg vil komme til dig
en dag,

naar vinden hænger dovent højt oppe over solen,
som et barn, der har leget sig træt-

jeg vil komme til dig paa stranden,
hvor klipperne ligger som løs varm aske paa
vandet,

og havet er som bleggrønt lys,
der forsigtigt er hældt ud over jorden-

den dag skal du ligge som en bølge,
af hvis rene skum
livet har skabt dine lænder-

jeg elsker dig ikke,
men vil komme til dig den dag
og trykke mine brændende øjne
mod dit dybe svale skød-

Sleep

I don't love you
but I will come to you
one day,

when the wind is hanging lazily high above the
sun,
like a child, tired from playing-

I will come to you on the beach
where the rocks lie like loose warm ash on
the water,

and the sea is like a pale green light,
carefully poured out over the Earth-

that day you will lie like a wave,
from whose clean foam
life has made your loins-

I don't love you,
but I will come to you that day
and press my burning eyes
against your deep cool lap-

Andre Nætter

       vi lagde vore garn og kroge
i stille blankt vand–
vi tog dem igen om morgenen–
saa kunde vandet være
som skraa grønne vægge,
der faldt ned i støv–

       nogle nætter fik vi god fangst–
da saa garnene ud
som svangre kvinders bug–
som store blanke kastanjer paa en snor
krøb krogene med fede daskende fisk
langsomt af vandet,
som saa var stille og blankt–
       andre nætter forliste vi garnene–

       vi lagde vore garn og kroge
om aftenen–
om natten gik vi med fugtige øjne
til byen–
vi var nyvaskede og i blaat tøj–

der gik de unge piger
med røde brændende kinder
som moden frugt–
       om morgenen
var der steder udenfor byen,
hvor græsset saa ud,
som om store dyr havde kæmpet der
den nat–
       andre nætter forliste vi garnene–

Other Nights

      we set our nets and hooks
in quiet smooth water-
we took them up again in the morning-
when the water could be
like slanted green walls,
falling down in dust-

      some nights we got a good catch-
then the nets looked
like a pregnant woman's belly-
like large glossy chestnuts on a string
the hooks with fat jumping fish
crawled slowly out of the water,
which then was quiet and smooth-
      other nights we lost the nets-

      we set our nets and hooks
in the evening-
in the night we went with moist eyes
to town-
we were fresh washed and in blue clothes-

there the young girls strolled
with red burning cheeks
like mature fruit-
      in the morning
there were places outside the town,
where the grass looked
as if large animals had fought there
that night-
      other nights we lost the nets-

Det

ikke den tanke,
at jeg endnu gaar paa stien
at jeg endnu har den trygge bjærgvæg
ved min side
at der gror blomster
og at græsset dæmper skridtets haardhed
at klippen udstraaler solens varme
men
det, at jeg ved,
at jeg kan træde fejl
at der er en afgrund
at jeg maa gaa sikkert,
og at bjærgvæggen ved min side
rykker nærmere kanten, jo længere jeg naar
at stien bliver haardere,
og skærvene skarpere
at græsset blir gult,
naar jeg kommer nær solen.

That

not the thought,
that I am still walking on the path
that I still have the secure mountain wall
at my side
that flowers are growing
and that the grass muffles the hard steps
that the rock radiates the sun's warmth
but
that, I know
that I can take a misstep
that there is an abyss
that I have to walk carefully,
and that the mountain wall at my side
is getting closer to the edge, the farther I get
that the path is getting harder,
and the stones sharper
that the grass gets yellow,
when I get closer to the sun.

Til Mine Forældre

jeg blev ikke det, I ventede
jeg blev alt det, I havde frygtet
I lod mig vokse op
næret ved jeres afsavn.
I opdrog mig med skjulte taarer
opdrog mig
til at leve jeres liv– fortsætte det
skal jeg sige:
saadan levede I; I gjorde ret
altsaa er det godt at leve saadan.
skal jeg?
eller skal jeg dræbe haabet i jer?
fortælle jer, at jeg ikke blev som I
at min verden er en anden end jeres,
min glæde,
min smerte en anden end jeres
vil I tro paa min tak til jer?
paa min tak til livet?
eller vil I sige:
han fik alt,
han tog alt af os,
og giver os intet tilbage,
andet end sorg og skuffelse.
jeg ved, I har ret, naar I siger det.
Jeg tror, jeg har ret, naar jeg gaar
                    til mit eget land.
men jeg gaar tøvende–
jeg gaar langsomt og tungt–
men jeg tror, jeg skal gaa.

To My Parents

I didn't become what you had expected
I became everything that you had feared
you let me grow up
nourished by your sacrifices.
you raised me with hidden tears
raised me
to live your life- continue it
Should I say:
that's how you lived; you did it right
so it's good to live that way.
should I?
or should I kill the hope in you?
tell you, that I did not become like you
that my world is another than yours,
my happiness,
my pain is another than yours
will you believe me when I thank you?
when I thank life?
or will you say:
he got everything,
he took everything from us,
and gives us nothing in return,
other than sorrow and disappointment.
I know, you are right, when you say it.
I think I am right when I go
                    to my own country.
but I go reluctantly-
I go slowly and heavily-
but I believe, I shall go.

Døden

hvorfor vi lever-
ja-
det hænder, at vi er saa glade, at vi synger
maaske blir vi saa lykkelige, saa glade,
at vi engang gaar vores vej,
af angst for at vi ikke mer skal høre
                    livets unge latter

Death

why we live-
well-
it happens, that we are so happy, that we sing
maybe we become so delighted, so happy,
that we some day will go our way,
out of fear that we no longer will hear
              life's young laughter

Læreaar

vore nætter
druknede i vinens sang
og kvindernes skød–

vi haabede,
at kraften vilde komme til os
som en herreløs hund
og lægge sig ved vore fødder–

til nogle af os kom længselen–
den rev vore skæbner løs
og bandt dem som trofæer
                        ved sit bælte–

Apprenticeship

our nights
drowned in the song of wine
and the laps of women—

we hoped
that the strength would come to us
like a dog without a master
and lie down at our feet—

longing came to some of us—
it ripped loose our fates
and tied them like trophies
                    to its belt—

Til En

       dig tør jeg ikke elske
din store blødtfavnende kærlighed
lægger sig som olje
paa min ungdoms urolige hav–

       mens jeg endnu beruset sover
mellem dine vuggende lemmer,
tømmer du legende
mit kogger for pile–

       dig vil jeg ikke elske
jeg vil se solen gennem brydende søer
       til de haarde toner fra min bues streng
vil jeg gaa ud at jage livet–

To One

       I don't dare to love you
your great soft embracing love
covers, like oil
the restless ocean of my youth–

       while I, still intoxicated, sleep
between your cradling limbs,
you playfully empty
the arrows from my quiver–

       I will not love you
I will see the sun through breaking waves
       to the hard tones from my bow's string
I will go forth to hunt life–

Generationer

ordene rakte sig
som beredvillige hænder imod os:
vent
se, I er unge,
se jeres smalle skuldre,
jeres ufærdige træk–
se livet staar undseeligt
som en fremmed blandt jer–
hør jeres tankers hurtige skridt,
naar de flygter for hinanden,
og vent–
lader I nu jeres ord
storme ud over verden,
for at splitte menneskenes ro,
i morgen vil I forgæves lokke dem tilbage–

vi tvivlede

Generations

the words stretched out
like willing hands toward us:
wait
look, you are young,
see your narrow shoulders,
your unfinished features—
see life standing bashful
like a stranger among you—
hear the quick steps of your thoughts,
when they run from each other,
and wait—
let your words
storm out over the world
to scatter the peace of man,
tomorrow you will try in vain to call them back—

we doubted

Med Lukkede Øjne

det er, som om
ingen strøm kan drukne mig
ingen sorg kvæle mig
helt-
det er som om
kærlighed kommer til mig
over alle have
fordi en blød streng altid svinger
i mig-

With Closed Eyes

it is, as if
no stream can drown me
no sorrow can choke me
completely-
it is as if
love comes to me
across all oceans
because a soft string is always swinging
in me-

Og Gud Talte

det var ikke gud–
hænderne legede, som børn i vejstøvet,
og hans øjne flagrede som hvide sommerfugle–
og han hviskede:
hvorfor gemmer I jeres drømme?
hvorfor bærer I ansigter foran jeres drømme?
i solen skulde I lægge dem–
i vinden skulde I brede dem ud,
paa vejene skulde I gaa nøgne under
                          jeres drømme,
at I kunde blive skønne, som de–
ikke med jeres øjne skulde I elske,
ikke gennem haardt glas skulde I se
                          trolddommen,
ikke gennem firkantede smil skulde
                          skønheden sive ud
og blive ædende draaber–
hvorfor gør I krigere af jeres hænder,
vogtere af jeres smil?
og hans øjne flagrede, og han talte:
o, at se hver enkelt drage ud
med sine drømme i oprakte hænder,
syngende mod solen og stormen:
elskede, her er alle mine drømme,
tag!
ve– ve over angsten–
ve– ve over angsten–
ikke lysten i jeres vagtsomme øjne
skulde I skænke jeres elskede,
ikke viden, dryppet ud i smil,
se jeres underlige længselsfulde hænder–
fyld jeres hænder med følsomhed,
og gaa til jeres elskede,
og sig:
her er alle mine drømme,
tag!

20

And God Spoke

it wasn't God-
the hands played, like children in the road dust,
and his eyes fluttered like white butterflies-
and he whispered:
why do you hide your dreams?
why do you carry faces in front of your dreams?
in the sun you should lay them-
in the wind you should spread them out,
on the roads you should walk naked under
                    your dreams.
that you could become lovely, like them
it's not with your eyes you should love,
not through hard glass you should see
                    witchcraft,
not through square smiles should
                    the beauty seep out
and become consuming drops-
why do you make warriors of your hands,
watchmen of your smiles?
and his eyes fluttered, and he spoke:
oh, to see each one go forth
with his dreams in upheld arms,
singing to the sun and storm:
beloved, here are all my dreams,
take them!
woe- woe to the fear-
woe- woe to the fear-
it's not the lust in your watchful eyes
that you should give to your beloved,
nor the knowledge, dripping out in smiles,
see your strange longing hands-
fill your hands with feeling,
and go to your beloved,
and say:
here are all my dreams,
take them!

Min Far

han vaklede
og jeg fangede hans øjne—
aah som vidunderlige tavse
hjælpeløse fuglehjærter var de
med den store smertes kraft,
som er kunsten,
straalende i et blankt hav—
o svagheden greb mig som en storm
og jeg slog—

en nat, hvor een lampe
samlede al ensomhed,
sprængtes frugten
og hans liv stormede ud i toner
og tvang himlen til graad—
og jeg bed i min tunge
afmægtig—

o, far
to hvide fugle
vogter godheden i min sjæl
med uovervindelig hellighed:
dine hænder—

My Father

he staggered
and I caught his eyes—
oh, like wonderful silent
helpless bird hearts they were
with the great pain's strength,
which is the art,
shining in a polished sea—
oh, the weakness grabbed me like a storm
and I struck—

one night, where one lamp
collected all the loneliness,
the fruit burst
and his life stormed out in tones
and forced the heaven to cry—
and I bit my tongue
powerless—

oh, father
two white birds
guard the goodness in my soul
with invincible holiness:
your hands—

Tal Ikke Til Mig

saa stille
saa stille
tal ikke!
meget meget forsigtigt
maa jeg gaa,
hvis jeg skal finde noget,
og alene maa jeg gaa,
hvis jeg skal finde noget—
endnu har jeg ingenting fundet
jeg har hverken
fundet mit hus
eller min elskede
eller mine marker—
de maa være
et sted, hvor jeg endnu ikke har været
jeg har allerede gaaet meget længe
maaske har jeg meget længe
endnu at gaa—
og helt alene maa jeg gaa
og saa forfærdelig forsigtigt
maa jeg gaa,
hvis jeg skal finde noget—
men jeg maa jo
finde et sted at være—
jeg maa jo have et hjem et sted—
jeg ved jo,
at jeg har mit hus
og mine marker et sted—
min elskede kan jo ikke vente altid—
jeg har allerede gaaet meget længe—
tal ikke til mig—
hvis jeg har alt for længe at gaa endnu,
blir det maaske for sent—
stille—stille!
jeg maa
finde mit hjem—

Don't Speak To Me

so quiet
so quiet
don't speak!
very very carefully
must I go,
if I am to find anything,
and I must go alone,
if I am to find anything-
so far I've found nothing
I have neither
found my house
or my beloved
or my fields-
they must be
some place, where I haven't been yet
I have already gone so far
maybe I have very far
yet to go-
and I must go all alone
and so very carefully
must I go,
if I am to find anything-
but I must
find a place to be-
I must have a home somewhere-
I know
that I have my house
and my fields somewhere-
my beloved can't wait forever-
I have already gone so far-
don't speak to me-
if I still have too far to go,
maybe it will be too late-
quiet-quiet!
I must
find my home-

Drengens Klage

hvor kan jeg gemme mig
hvor kan jeg gemme mig,
o i nat vil de alle komme
vil de alle komme fra hele verden—
o findes der ikke
et eneste skjulested
bare et eneste skjulested
til mig
i nat—
jeg er saa bange
jeg dør af angst,
naar ingen synger i hele verden
om natten—

o hvor kan jeg gemme mig
gemme mig bare i nat—
alle de store sange
er døde hjemme
hjemme er ikke flere store sange
nu synger de kun smaa sange
hjemme—

o jeg dør af angst,
naar ingen synger i hele Verden
om natten—

The Boy's Lament

where can I hide
where can I hide,
oh, tonight they will all come
from the whole world they will all come—
oh, isn't there somewhere
one single hiding place
just one single hiding place
for me
tonight—
I am so afraid
I am dying of fear,
when nobody in the whole world sings
in the night—

oh, where can I hide
hide for just tonight—
all of the great songs
are dead at home
at home there are no more great songs
now they only sing small songs
at home—

oh, I am dying of fear,
when nobody in the whole world sings
in the night—

Nomader

som nyfødte børns fødder
er jeres øjne under længselen–
gaa! gaa!
langs de underligt talende floder–
som føder skovene,
og fylder dem med svar–
o, skovene,
der kryster floderne
som lyttende melankolske slanger,
og trækker himlen ned over sig
med døve urokkelige arme–
gaa!, maaske finder I der
en vældig kvinde
med herlige syngende fødder
og hvide øjne!, eller
bjærge af sovende mænd
med røde brændende sanser
imellem sig som baal–
eller rædselsgrebne børn
med ansigter af haardtbrændt ler–,
og hænderne knugende om smaa plettede sten–
eller I finder den fede gud,
hvis taarer hamrer syndflodsglæde
mod sumpplanters haarde blade,
hvis smaa øjne smiler,
mens taarerne trommer som fortvivlede tænder
hurtigere og hurtigere–
gaa!
altid finder I noget– (ikke helbredelsen)
ser I ikke, at jeres sygdom
er større end alle andre–
o, mange er I,
I, som har smitten–
gaa!
og giv jeres uendelige uro over jorden,
altid finder I noget!

Nomads

like the feet of new-borns
your eyes are longing-
go! go!
along the strangely speaking rivers-
which feed the forests,
filling them with answers-
oh, the forests,
which embrace the rivers
like listening melancholy snakes,
pulling down the sky
with deaf and resolute arms-
go!, maybe there you will find
a great woman
with wonderful singing feet
and white eyes!, or
mountains of sleeping men
with red burning senses
between them like fires-
or terrified children
with faces of hard fired clay,
and hands clutching small spotted stones-
or you will find the fat god,
whose tears beat the torrent of joy
against the hard leaves of the marsh plants,
whose small eyes smile,
while the tears drum like desperate teeth
faster and faster-
go!
you will always find something- (not the cure)
don't you see, that your disease
is greater than all others-
oh, many are you,
you, who are infected-
go!
and spread your eternal anxiety over the Earth,
you will always find something!

Blod

en søndag morgen
gav du blod
til din mest elskede drøm—

dit legeme sang om stor lykke,
drømmen døde,
og du fødte mig—

mor, den døde,
drømmen—
det var mig, du fødte,
o du gav drømmen dit blod—

mor!
blod!
mit hjerte er ikke en sten—
mit hjerte
er
ikke sten—
o, jeg ser:
blod er ikke dejlig elskov—
blod— blod
er kobberlænker—
kære mor, ikke jeg er drømmen—
mor— hvorfor snor dine evigt
                    rastløse fingre
taalsome lokker—
for mig?
hvorfor ser din sjæls øjne
altid vaagende
endeløse marker, hvide af ben?
hvorfor bøjer ørneryg knæ
for uværdige guder?
hvorfor græder du— mor—
for mig?

Blood

one Sunday morning
you gave blood
to your most beloved dream-

your body sang of great happiness-,
the dream died,
and you gave birth to me-

mother, it died,
the dream-
it was me, you gave birth to,
oh, you gave the dream your blood-

mother!
blood!
my heart is not a stone-
my heart
is
not stone-
oh, I see:
blood is not delightful love-
blood- blood
is a copper chain-
dear mother-, I am not the dream-
mom- why are your ever restless
                    fingers twisting
patient curls-
for me?
why do your soul's eyes see
always vigilant
endless fields, white of bone?
why does the eagle's back bow
for unworthy gods?
why are you crying- mother-
for me?

kære mor,
saa du ikke at drømmen døde?
min mor!
elskede– rejs dig–se vejen!
(o se ikke altid
flaskerne
grinende kvinder
sult–
se ikke altid gruset, stenene–)
se vejen!
se den vej, som jeg gaar, som du fødte
søndagen, da dit skød var livets
                syngende mund–

mor–hvorfor ønsker du mig
søvnen
mætheden
usaarligheden?
giv mig kraft, mor,
af det mod, du fik
hin søndag,
da du ikke saa,
at din skønneste drøm døde–
og mor– mor
engang,
naar jeg har fundet vejens halespids
dybt inde i det underste land,
skal vi mødes
og som en dobbelt draabe flyde ud i søen,
som er livets øje!
kære mor–

o, mor–
at du gav drømmen dit blod–
o, stakkels mor, elskede mor–
store mor–

dear mother,
didn't you see that the dream died?
my mother!
beloved- stand up- see the path!
(oh, don't always see
the bottles
laughing women
hunger-
don't always see the gravel, the stones-)
see the path!
see the path, that I travel, that you bore
that Sunday, when your womb was life's
                        singing mouth-

mother- why do you wish for me
sleep
satiety
invulnerability?
give me strength, mother,
of that courage, you found
that Sunday,
when you didn't see,
that your most beautiful dream died-
and mother- mother
sometime,
when I have found the tail of the path
deep inside the lowermost land,
we shall meet
and like a double drop flow out into the sea,
which is the eye of life!
dear mother-

Oh, mother-
that you gave the dream your blood-
oh, poor mother, beloved mother-
great mother-

Det Underste Land (til fannie hurst)

o stor lykke
stor lykke har de faaet,
som er født i det underste land–
overalt kan I se dem
vandrende
elskende
grædende–
overalt gaar de,
men i deres hænder bærer de smaa ting
fra det underste land–
o større end alle lande
herligere
er det underste–
opad vrider jorden sig
i en spids–
og nedad
udad synker det tunge
levende blod
ind i det underste land–
smalle forsigtige fødder
og tynde lemmer
og ren er luften
over de aabne opadstigende veje–
i lukkede aarer
brænder længselen hos dem,
der er født oppe under himlen–
men o
I skulde gaa til det underste land!
o I skulde se folket fra det underste land,
hvor blodet flyder frit mellem alle–
mænd–
kvinder–
børn–
hvor glæden og fortvivlelsen og elskoven
tunge og fuldmodne

The Lowermost Land (to Fannie Hurst)

oh great happiness
great happiness they have received,
who were born in the lowermost land-
you can see them everywhere
wandering
loving
crying-
they go everywhere,
but in their hands they carry small things
from the lowermost land
oh greater than all lands
more delightful
is the lowermost-
the Earth twists itself upwards
in a point-
and downwards
outwards sinks the heavy
living blood
into the lowermost land
narrow careful feet
and thin limbs
and pure is the air
over the open ascending paths-
in closed veins
the longing is burning in those,
who were born up under the sky-
but oh
you should go to the lowermost land!
oh, you should see the people from the lowermost
land,
where the blood flows freely between all-
men-
women-
children-
where joy and despair and love,
heavy and mature,

straaler i alle farver mod jorden–
o jorden er hemmelighedsfuld som en pande
i det underste land–

overalt kan I se dem
vandrende
elskende
grædende–
deres ansigter er lukkede,
og paa indersiden af deres sjæle sidder jord
fra det underste land–

shine in all colors towards the Earth-
oh, the Earth is secretive as a brow
in the lowermost land

you can see them everywhere
wandering
loving
crying-
their faces are closed,
and on the inside of their souls there is soil
from the lowermost land-

Sang

gudebarn, som jeg elsker!
hvormange skal jeg slaa?

skal jeg altid komme
til dit smil, som siger:
stakkels dræbende gudemenneske?
de kan jo ikke lide
kun bløde—
kun prøve—
kun dø—
hvorlænge gudebarn?
skal mit solhjerte altid strejfe
altid komme
altid være for langt borte
til at kunne høres
af dig o gudebarn, som jeg elsker?

aah
flodgraad
sanggraad—
hulkende hulkende
vished om alle nætter
og alle bølger—
altid leve
mellem døde menneskesmerter uden melodi
uden lidelse
uden hellighed?
gudebarn, som jeg elsker
hvormange skal jeg slaa?

du har min tone
i glasbløde havstængeltanker om din hals—
smil ikke mer!
mit solhjerte vil gaa ind
i din mund nu

Song

God-child, who I love!
how many shall I slay?

shall I always come
to your smile, that says:
the poor killing God-people?
they cannot even suffer
only bleed-
only try-
only die-
how long God-child?
must my sun-heart always roam
always come
always be too far away
to be heard
by you oh God-child, who I love?

oh
river of tears
song of tears-
sobbing sobbing
certainty of all the nights
and all the waves-
always living
between dead human pain without a melody
without suffering
without sanctity?
God-children, who I love
how many shall I slay?

you have my tone
in glass soft sea stalk thoughts around your neck-
smile no more!
my sun-heart will enter
your mouth now

og skænke dig det sidste raab
elskede gudebarn!
mine kurver er fulde
vi lever evigt bagefter
vi har allerede glemt
solhjerte
menneskedrab
gudebørn–

and give you the last cry
beloved God-child!
my baskets are full
we live for ever after
we have already forgotten
sun-heart
genocide
God-child-

Afsked

en makrelstime er en regn
af undervejsdræbende
strygende sortrygge
havet har ingen lyd–
mit
hjærtes læber er to
makrelrygge
du er et offer–
havet hvisker retningen
med stor fart
tramp tramp tramp
i dit hjærte
jeg ved det–
du faar mit had for det

Departure

a mackerel school is a storm
of killers on the move
streaking black backs
the sea has no sound—
my
heart's lips are two
mackerel backs
you are a victim—
the sea whispers the direction
with great speed
stamp stamp stamp
in your heart
I know it—
you have my hatred for it

Morgentime

paa himlens dybe
bund af nat
ligger som kul
alle elskovsgnisterne–
stille fløj de
een efter een
sorte perler paa
himlens bund–

Jeg, Den Udvalgte,
er i nat blot
søvnvogteren
dødssværdet
for Den Store Kærligheds
dør–
under den matgyldne
portal med
korslagte ben
sidder jeg vaagen
med vogtersværdet paa
mit knæ–

himlens sæd rinder gennem
alle tage–
bag døren, hvor den
store kærlighed sover,
hører jeg uden at lytte
de store fugles hvisken
om duftløse vidunderlige
blomster–
hver ild er
død, og
de hvide sletter trykker
al vind indtil sig
i voldsom søvn–

Morning Hour

on heaven's deep
bottom of night
lying like coal
all sparks of love-
quietly they flew
one after one
black pearls on
heaven's bottom

I, The Chosen,
tonight am just
the guard of sleep
the sword of death
before The Great Love's
door-
under the dull golden
door with
crossed legs
I sit awake
with the guard's sword on
my knee

the seed of heaven runs through
all the roofs-
behind the door, where the
great love sleeps,
I hear without listening
the great birds' whispering
about scentless wonderful
blossoms-
every fire is
dead, and
the white plains pull down
all the wind
in violent sleep-

sjakalerne holder vejret
stirrende mod himlen
med blinde øjne-
ingen smiler-
ingen spejle dugges-
DEN STORE KÆRLIGHED
SOVER-

silkebløde jomfrutaager
glider atter over
susende munde og
drømmeløse skød
og mellem
den store kærligheds læber
spindes strængelaag-

ingen vil kende
nogen efter
denne nat-
og alle træk vil
være smeltet,
naar en morgen kommer-

naar nattens
purpurjolle blomstrer,
skal ingen være udvalgt,
og min dronning skal
have mistet sin krone-

the jackals hold their breath
staring toward heaven
with blind eyes-
nobody smiles-
no mirror is fogged-
THE GREAT LOVE
SLEEPS

silk soft virgin mists
glide again over
rushing mouths and
dreamless laps
and between
the great love's lips
is spun a cover of string

nobody will know
anyone after
this night-
and all features will
be melted,
when a morning comes

when the night's
purple lilies bloom,
no one shall be chosen,
and my queen shall
have lost her crown-

Sjælens Sang (fragment)

naar budbringeren kommer,
og hadet falder fra
mine træk som
dagens tørre hunger,
vil menneskene blændes af
en skønhed, der sprænger alt—
og de vil bedække
deres aasyn og mumle:
„alt gaar under,
døden er over os"
men deres drømme vil
rejse sig og vidne:
at hjemlandet er
en eneste solgydende opfyldelse
af det højeste,
een nat for alle
af evig klarhed,
bygget over udødelige
skaberdrømmes skuldre—

og gennem mit hjemlands græs
sukker det
lykketungt
under den ringestes fod:
„hellige nat, hvor
solen har fundet sin brud"

jeg ser:
mit had var hvidt som dagen—
men mine drømme skal bære
altet—

Song of the Soul (fragment)

when the messenger comes,
and the hate falls from
my features like
the day's dry hunger,
then humans will be blinded by
a beauty, that breaks everything-
and they will cover
their countenance and mumble:
"everything goes under,
death is over us"
but their dreams will
arise and bear witness:
that the homeland is
a solitary sun-shining fulfilment
of the highest,
one night for all
of eternal clarity
built on the shoulders of
immortal creator's dreams.

and through my homeland's grass
it sighs
so happy
under the foot of the most humble:
"holy night, where
the sun has found his bride"

I see:
my hate was as white as the day-
but my dreams shall carry
the world

o, hvad er jeg andet
end min mægtigste drøm—
og, hvad er den største og
den ringeste andet
end deres mægtigste, mest
ubekymrede drøm!

naar budbringeren kommer,
vil jeg aande mod hans bryst:
aldrig, aldrig er
jeg ophørt at se dette!
og naar jeg løfter øjnene
vil *han* aabne muren
og atter nævne mig
i mit hjemland—

Oh, what am I other
than my mightiest dream-
and, what is the greatest
and the least other than
their mightiest, most
carefree dream!

when the messenger comes,
I will breathe against his breast:
never, never have
I stopped seeing this!
and when I lift my eyes
he will open the gate
and again name me
in my homeland-

Ung Martyr

en fremmed stjernetaage
over himlen
nærmer sig jorden–

lad stjernen tale selv–
stjæl ikke dens skær
og dens dyrtpansrede frihed–

hvem
kan sige en stjernes maal?
hvem
tør hindre dens flugt?
og hvem
tør tale før sejrens tavshed?

men du, som vil
dø en herlig død,
tag stjernens skjoldtegn
i renede hænder, og
din død vil
blive en stjernes nat–

Young Martyr

a strange star cloud
over the heaven
approaches Earth

let the star speak-
don't steal its glow
and its costly armored freedom-

who
can say a star's goal?
who
dares hinder its flight?
and who
dares speak before victory's silence?

but you, who will
die a splendid death,
take the star's coat of arms
in clean hands, and
your death will
be a stars night-

Tidlig Morgen

min barndoms klipper er bare og hede—
min barndoms hav har tusind strømme,
          men een retning—
af min barndoms hav har jeg lært at
          elske til alle tider—
i hver fod, hver ryg, hver bøjet fyrr,
          hver knastør fjældblomst
elsker jeg saltet og heden til alle tider—
i stjernetaarer, stjernetaarer alene
er saltet og min barndoms hede sten—

Early Morning

my childhood's rocks are bare and hot
my childhood's sea has thousands of currents,
              but just one direction-
from my childhood's sea I have learned to
              love at all times-
in every foot, every ridge, every bending fir,
              every bone dry mountain flower
I love the salt and heat at all times-
in starry tears, only in starry tears
is the salt and my childhood's hot stones-

Koldt; Men Rent

jeg har fundet
at jeg ikke er fuldendt
som jeg havde troet—
og jeg har fundet
at det er uden betydning—

jeg har fundet
at min kærlighed
til ham, hun eller dem
er uvæsentlig—
jeg har fundet
at jeg intet er uden en stemme
og at den ikke er min—

jeg har fundet
at "jeg" er et nødvendigt stedord—
-at skabe
af alles magt i mig
er min pligt—
jeg har lært
at det fineste redskab rammer finest.

Cold; But Clean

I have found
that I'm not perfect
like I had believed-
and I have found
that it doesn't matter-

I have found
that my love
to him, her or them
is not important-
I have found
that I am nothing without a voice
and that it isn't mine-

I have found
that "I" is a necessary pronoun-
-to create
from everyone's power in me
is my obligation-
I have learned
that the sharpest tool cuts best.

Mit Liv

jeg mærker din nærhed, o Herre–
jeg taler til dig, Herre, uden frygt, for min sjæl
vakler mod dødens hvile–
er det der, du venter mig, Herre?
og jeg vil gaa i dette nu, saaledes, som jeg gik,
da min verdens elskede kaldte mig over
                havene;
er døden de tre skridt, som endnu mangler i,
at jeg hører din stemme, Herre?
eller er dette mit liv en af Dine gerninger?
er min sidste sluknende angst Din vilje
                fra det fjerne–
Herre, jeg spørger ikke for at udraabe,
at jeg kender dit sind–
Mægtige, dig spørger jeg,
fordi verden spænder mig i en klædning,
som aldrig var min–
Herre, er det Din?, da gør mig anderledes–
nu er den undergang for min eneste vilje–
jeg mærker din nærhed, o, Herre–
og døden hindrer ikke mere min længsels fod–
men vis din vilje, Herre,
før mit øje er blindet af en vind,
som aldrig var min,
og jeg maa leve uden at ane dit blik,
omend i den fjerneste time–
og Herre, Herre,
jeg ængstes for de dræbende mil,
du har lagt imellem disse timer,
hvor jeg mærker din nærhed–
o, Herre, jeg taler til dig uden frygt,
men ikke der– der vil jeg ikke dø–
da affører jeg mig hellere denne fremmede
                dragt og
gaar under–
Herre, er *det* din vilje?
Herre, din nærhed er tavs, som jeg

My Life

I feel Your closeness, oh Lord-
I speak to You, Lord, without fear, for my soul
lurches toward death's rest-
is it there, You await me, Lord?
and I will go at once, just as I went
when the love of my world called me over
                the seas;
is death the three steps, still needed,
for me to hear Your voice, Lord?
or is this my life one of Your works?
is my last fading fear Your will
                from afar-
Lord, I don't ask just to proclaim,
that I know Your mind-
All Mighty, I ask You,
because the world is wrapping me in clothing
that was never mine-
Lord, is it Yours?, then make me different-
now it is the ruin of my only wish-
I feel Your closeness, oh Lord-
and death no longer hinders my longing feet-
but show Your will, Lord,
before my eye is blinded by a wind,
which was never mine,
and I must live without knowing Your glance,
even in the most distant hour-
and Lord, Lord,
I worry about the killing miles,
You have put between these hours,
where I feel Your closeness-
oh, Lord, I speak to You without fear,
but not there- there I will not die-
then I would rather take off this strange clothing
and submit-
Lord, is that Your will?
Lord, Your closeness is silent, like me-

Glimt—Varslende—Flygtet

usynlig– straalende favner min væren
unærmelig maanens hellige fod–
lydløst– frembrydende rinder
det altfor sky's nomade,
snor sig det altfor dyrebare's krone
om sin egen ring–

uafvidende skal jeg bortgives
aldrig beprøvet og intet lovende–
min længsel brænder sig selv–
et flammende taarn at ses af ingen–
og øverst
min blusels lyre– venter– venter–
bævende for styrken– uanet– uanet–
strængene smelter hede draaber,
græder glødende vanvid,
seende, spaaende–
ingen skal ane det:
-det sprøde, det som aldrig
har blomstret forgæves,
som aldrig har grublet
og aldrig har villet,
det altfor sky
og det altfor dyrebare,
som aldrig har trodset
og aldrig svævet,
det af alle
skal kende barneguden, naar han
                                    kommer–
lyren- bævende-
skal sprænge hans bud
og elske hans læber-
det nye vanvid, det altfor rene,
skal hviske sejren mod hans skulder-

Flash- Warning- Fled

invisibly-radiantly my being embraces
unapproachably the moon's holy foot-
silently- rising into sight
the way too shy nomad,
winds its way too costly crown
around its own ring-

unknowingly I shall be given away
never tried and promising nothing -
my longing burns itself-
a flaming tower to be seen by no one-
and over all
my shame's lyre- waiting- waiting
trembling for strength, unsuspected- unsuspected
the strings melt hot drops,
cry glowing madness,
seeing, foretelling-
no one shall suspect it:
the brittleness, that which never
has flowered in vain,
which has never pondered
and has never wanted,
the way too shy
the way too costly,
which has never defied
and never drifted,
that of all
shall know the Child-God, when he
                              comes-
the lyre, trembling-
shall sound his message
and love his lips-
the new madness, the way too clean,
shall whisper victory against his shoulder-

Tanke

alt legemligt
er sjælens udtryk–
den rene sjæl
gør alting helligt–
den svage sjæl
rafler uskyldigt
om andres skæbne–
der findes intet
urent i menneskets kød,
og al skabelse
er ogsaa sjælens
alene–

Thought

everything bodily
is an expression of the soul-
the pure soul
makes everything holy-
the weak soul
wagers innocently
with the fate of others-
nothing impure is found
in the body of man,
and all creation
is also the soul's
alone-

Sang

—fløjt klingende din vise om en
          gylden dag,
klag din knugende smærte i moll—
sandheden hvisker nynnende melodien
i krattet bag grøften,
i stuens mørke—
          glæd dig, lyttende vandrer,
over harmoniens naadegave,
flygt, ilsomt og stille,
for tonernes dystre kamp—
stemmer og toner besvarer, vandrer,
knivskarpt dit spørgende smil—

Song

—whistle sonorously your ballad about a
                    golden day,
moan your crushing pain in minor-
the truth whispers, humming, the melody
in the thicket behind the ditch,
in the darkness of the room-
            rejoice, listening wanderer,
over harmony's grace,
run, quickly and quietly,
for the tones' somber struggle-
voices and tones answer, wanderer,
knife-sharp, your questioning smile-

Rids

viben skriger
en cirkel sort
skriger en kurve hvid
i luften–
saltengen drejer sig
grøn–graa vaad
med et lukket æg
i midten–

havet glider rødmende
ind i solens ild,
aften aander salt
mod morgens vind–
en maage forsvinder i sløret sus,
fiskeren vaagner til dag–

Sketch

the lapwing cries
a circle black
cries a curve white
in the air-
the salt marsh is turning
green-gray wet
with a closed egg
in the middle-

the sea glides blushingly
into the sun's fire,
the evening breathes salt
against the morning's breeze-
a gull disappears in a veiled rush,
the fisherman wakes to the day-

Lav Horisont

regngraa stormvind
trykker vintersæds blaagrønne spirer
mod sorte knolde–
markerne bølger tungt,
dunkel–grønne haar følger
i nikkende dans stormens
isnende strøg over krybende muld–
himlen kaster sig sort udad
mod havet–
grønne spirer nikker i takt
flimrende under stormens slør–

Low Horizon

rain gray storm winds
push the winter seed's blue-green sprouts
against black clods-
the fields wave heavily,
dark-green hair follows
in a nodding dance the storm's
icy touch over creeping top soil-
heaven throws itself black, outwards
toward the sea-
green sprouts nod in time
flickering under the storm's veil-

Rødt og Sort

de grønne blade blir gule–
stormene river
maaned efter maaned–
gul–røde blade klamrer sig til sorte grene–
langsomt vrider regnen stilkene løse–
saften staar stille i roden–

under jagende himmel
sover mulden sin hvile–
grønne menneskehjærter sortner–
menneskenes storme blødende nærmer sig–
forvirrings regn siver nat og dag–
hjærtets love mørner–
efteraars straalende pragt
vandrer i døde kolonner
gennem menneskenes byer–
solen er fjernest nu–

Red and Black

the green leaves turn yellow-
the storms sweep
month after month-
yellow-red leaves cling to the black branches-
slowly the rain twists the stems loose-
the sap stays quietly in the root-

under a driving sky
the sleeping soil rests-
green human hearts turn black-
the human storm approaches, bleeding-
the rain of confusion falls night and day-
the heart's laws soften-
autumn's radiant splendor
wanders in dead columns
through the cities of man-
the sun is farthest now-

Se!

se solen, solen,
føl luften i det levende bryst,
græsset under foden i glæde, glæde,
endnu lever du jo!
o, se, solen staar op,
se, dit barn sover,
– se !
endnu lever du jo,
din kvinde glæder sig i dit hus–
–fyld dine øjne med det varme, herlige
                    lys,
levende broder!

See!

see the sun, the sun,
feel the breeze in the living breast,
the grass under foot in happiness, happiness,
you are still alive!
oh, see, the sun rises,
see, your child sleeps,
-see !
-you are still alive,
your woman is happy in your house
-fill your eyes with the warm, delightful
                    light,
living brother!

Bøn

magter, som styrer himlen og jorden
solen og stormen og havet,
magter, som styrer, usynligt for blikket,
menneskenes færden og liv,
magter, som styrer, usynligt for sjælen,
trældom og nød, skælvende glæde,
krige og rædsler, skændsel og synd,
magter, jeg tigger i pine,
giv mig lys for mit virke,
magter, lad mig ikke dø unyttig,
mægtige, brænd eders mærke
dybt ind i mit vaklende sind–

Prayer

powers, that rule the Heaven and Earth
the sun, and the storm and the sea,
powers, that rule, invisible to the eye,
man's movements and life,
powers, that rule, invisible to the soul,
bondage and want, shivering joy,
war and terror, scandal and sin,
powers, I beg in pain,
give me light for my work,
powers, don't let me die in vain,
great powers, burn your mark
deep into my wavering mind-

Brødre

brødre i livets taager,
brødre i nøden paa jorden,
det forfærdelige findes,
skændselen lever i pragt,
døden vandrer ved vor side
saaende mørke og stank,
brødre, skabt til mensker,
alting har en sandhed
lysende skarp og klar,
alting har sin lov
ubrydelig fra dybet til det højeste,
den frie menskesjæl
har øjne skabt til lys,
dybt i nødens grave
brænder evig sandhed,
selv paa livets bund
bliver løgnen aldrig ild,
selv i skændselens dynd
gløder menskets lov
ufattelig som gud–

Brothers

brothers in life's mist,
brothers in need on Earth,
the terror is here,
scandal lives in glory,
death wanders at our side
sowing dark and foulness,
brothers, created as men,
everything has a truth
shining sharp and clear,
everything has its laws
unbreakable from the deep to the highest,
the free soul of man
has eyes created for the light,
deep in the grave of need
the eternal truth burns,
even at the bottom of life
the lie never turns to flame,
even in scandal's mire
the law of man glows
incomprehensible like God-

Marts

sneen ligger
fast og hvid–
havet straaler
sommerblaat–
flammende sol
og isklar luft
brænder i trætte øjne–
havfugle yngler,
hæse stære skriger–
natten kommer
sort og dyb–
baade følger
stimende sild–
over landet i vest
gnistrer en stjærne grønt–

March

the snow lies
firm and white-
the sea shines
summer blue-
flaming sun
and ice clear air
burn in tired eyes
sea birds breed,
hoarse starlings cry-
the night comes
black and deep
boats follow
shoaling herring
over the land in the west
a star flickers green

Eight English poems from Black God's Stone

Portrait

when sleeping
I seek my princess-,

in the morning
I break all the flowers-,

in the sun
I build my aloneness-,

towards night
I carve out the future,-

my life I spare-
my death
shall never exist-

In the glade

my fate
has no shadows
no home
and no friendly lake -
no whispering trees
and no female moon -
my fate
has no poems
no caressing fire,
and my way has
no polished end at last -
- you think
me the waiting poet
I am not -

my fate shall not change -
I shall never
control my hissing voice -
I shall
never bring to my people
tied-up the broad-scaled fish of wisdom -
my people
shall never lift from my hands
the glowing gifts of my god -
never shall I leave the forests,
my fate shall never roar from the lustrious spires
of clearness -
my fate shall not change -

I am the dark-faced hunter,
I am hunting the arrows
from the unseen suns -,
I am hunting the coiling cues
from the waiting earth -
I throw my prey on the waters -
for the sharp-eyed to catch,
for the able to sow -
don't send your beggars to me -,
my mercy is gone -
don't send your rulers to me,
my humbleness is gone
if they come, the begging rulers,
I'll take them to the Stone in the glade
and betray them there -
if my fettered brothers
do seek me deep in the forest,
I'll show them the craving of their re-born God -,
I will lend them
my eye and my spear -

but my dearest prey
I have thrown on the waters,
to feed my children -
I am the dark-faced hunter,
I throw my gold on the waters -

Proposal

this is me-
this is, what I
demand
from the mate,
which is to be mine:

when she is near me,
we shall be born from god-,
when I am with her,
we shall beget the prince,
for whom the world is waiting

when I leave her,
to risk my life with my icy fate,
her pride shall conquer
easily her womb

when I beg her to heal
my tired-to-death despair,
she,
with steel-hard courage,
shall show me again and again
the way which may hold out
the destruction of me,
her man
her eye
shall be the merciless
killer of my will to die
her foot
shall be the burning sceptre
to my victorious joy
her life
shall be the voice
of my blood
I shall call her
my woman

My evening has come

here I sit -
looking into my flickering fire
before me -
outside the tent
my enemies are whispering
to each other -
I was the victor always -
I could never be conquered -
they could not touch me -

here I sit -
the all-embracing serenity
on me -
always my deepest desire
was fulfilled -
my success is still as clean, as new ice -
I was always able to take
my soul's want -
I was able
to make of my self what I wanted -,
what I must -

I could never be conquered -
I was always the victor -
here I sit -
with my legs crossed, looking
with far-off eyes into my own fire -
outside the tent
the hatred goes on whispering -
to night I shall be murdered -
I -, the victor -,
I who couldn't be conquered -
my unpierceable quietude embraces everything
like the first mother -
here I sit -
with my tent around me -
my evening has come -

To the earth

now, mother -,
I have covered my face into your bosom -
now, mother -,
I can have rest a short time, completely -
now, mother -,
my eyes are closed upon yours, closed too –

mother -,
you gave me the power of giving the comfort
which alone is nourishing and bright -
but, mother -,
I would only once give, what you have given me,
and not being forced to take back my gifts as
hitherto
for the sake of your purity -, my mother -

but now,
mother -,
my eyes are closed upon yours, closed too -
now, mother -,
I can have rest a short time, completely -

God of all nature

god of all nature,
if you would take
me in your unseen hand
to be filled or to fill!
god of all nature,
and you will
or you will not, and
I am still yours,
a foot in the dark,
god of all nature

Song

I have no need of women,
why should I
why should you?
I have no need of men,
why should I
why should you?
—sometimes I want to love,
then I set off
far away, or not far,
for where love is
why should I
why should you?
it is fine to seek what you want,
fine to wander far or not far,
to seek what you want,
it is fine to be always proud -
why should I
why should you?

Eulogy for Gustaf Munch-Petersen

"Voluntarios Internacionales de la Libertad"- Freedom's International Volunteers, this proud Spanish name for the International Brigade during the Spanish Civil War, 1936-39, was not carried by anyone with a greater or more fervent right than Gustaf Munch-Petersen.

I met Gustaf early in the year of 1938, in a training camp for Scandinavians, where he held a leading position as a steward or "Police Commissioner". He was popular and respected, but he was a loner among these Scandinavians, for whom the question was simple and obvious: Fascism must be defeated. Gustaf was an intellectual, and the idea of meeting violence with violence was a real problem, and contemporary problems were deeply personal. He hated violence, but saw no alternative than to meet the rampaging, sabre rattling Fascists with violence— and he didn't just approve of this in theory, but put his own life on the line as well...

In 1943, in the Danish concentration camp in Horserød, I met several comrades who had fought in the Spanish War for Freedom. One of them recounted how Gustaf had fallen:

It was during Franco's great offensive in the spring of 1938. With an overwhelming show of men and equipment, the Fascists pushed forward to the Mediterranean coast. The government put all disposable forces in to stop them, but in vain. It was obvious to everyone, that this was the decisive battle. All of the International units participated in the battle, and new Spanish divisions were formed in haste. But poorly equipped, without reserves or heavy weapons, the government forces could not hold their position. Soon surrounded, and with no knowledge of the enemy position, and no internal communication, the government troops, still fighting, fell back in groups. Depression had affected all of them: they felt that defeat was upon them, and they saw the shadow of fascism fall across Europe.

Gustaf, his comrades said, had, during the retreat, become despondent over the developments. He had fought bravely and tirelessly, but a desperation had taken hold in him, something they had not seen before. There were only about ten men in their group.

Suddenly Gustaf refused to retreat further. His comrades explained the obvious, that just a handful of men could not stop an army.

— They *must* be stopped, he continued to say. For him it was not a question of what they *could* do, but of what they *must* and *should* do. When the fascists overran the little group, Gustaf held his position. Those who did get away heard, for some time, his firefight with the enemy. They never saw him again ...

"They must be stopped". That sentence echoed in the ears of a condemned man in the spring of 1945, while he sat on death row in the police station, waiting for his sentence to be carried out. It was at the end of March, at the same time that Gustaf, 7 years earlier, had fallen, and the condemned patriot was one of Gustaf's friends. "They *must* be stopped". That sentence helped the condemned get through a crushing feeling of loneliness, which probably affects all who are sacrificed to a superior power. And when he saw before him the execution squad's threatening rifles, the sight was transformed to that of Gustaf, who alone lay and fired at the approaching enemy:

They *must* be stopped!

Leo W. Kari

Bibliography

Works published during his lifetime
det nøgne menneske (naked man):Copenhagen 1932-poetry
simon begynder(simon begins): Copenhagen 1933-novel
det underste land(the lowermost land): Copenhagen 1933-poetry
mod jerusalem(towards Jerusalem): Copenhagen 1934-poetry
nitten digte(nineteen poems): Copenhagen 1937-poetry

Works published after his death
Udvalgte Digte(Selected Poems): Copenhagen 1938
Udvalgte Digte(Selected Poems): 2nd. edition Copenhagen 1946
Samlede Skrifter(Complete Works): Copenhagen 1959*
Udvalgte Digte(Selected Poems): 3rd. edition Copenhagen 1962
Samlede Skrifter(Complete Works): 2nd edition Copenhagen 1967
Samlede Skrifter(Complete Works): 3rd edition Copenhagen 1988

Books about Gustaf Munch-Petersen
Gustafs ansigter(The Faces of Gustaf): Martine Cardel Gertsen
2003
Malerier og digte(paintings and poems):Martine Gertsen,Erik
Hagens
2008
Gustaf Munch-Petersen og Den Spanske Borgerkrig
(Gustaf Munch-Petersen and the Spanish Civil War):Ole Sohn
2007

*includes the previously unpublished manuscripts: "black god's
stone"(English poems), and "solen finns" (Swedish poems). With
an introduction by Torben Brostrøm.

The most comprehensive bibliography of the works of Gustaf
Munch-Petersen is found in *Gustafs Ansigter.*

www.ingramcontent.com/pod-product-compliance
Lightning Source LLC
Chambersburg PA
CBHW051815040426
42446CB00007B/691